JOURNEYS THROUGH TIME

A COMPREHENSIVE WORLD HISTORY GUIDE FOR UPSC ASPIRANTS

SANKATALA JHAATIN

ISBN 979-8-89363-406-8

Contents

THIS BOOK CONTAINS ONLY IMPORTANT CHAPTERS
WHICH ARE COVERED IN UPSC

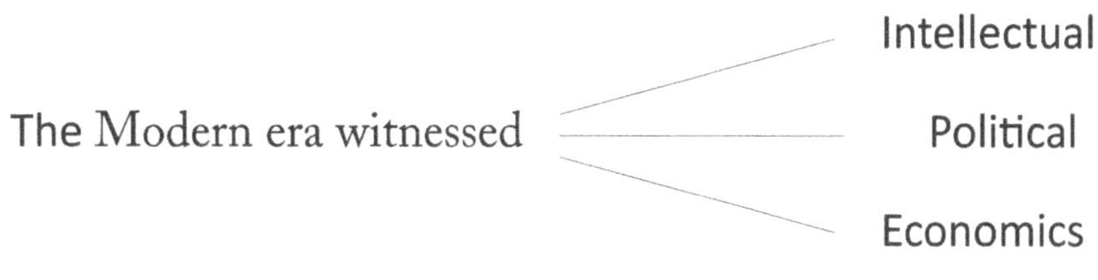

During the pre-modern era [15th to 18th centuries]

Basic Divisions of World History

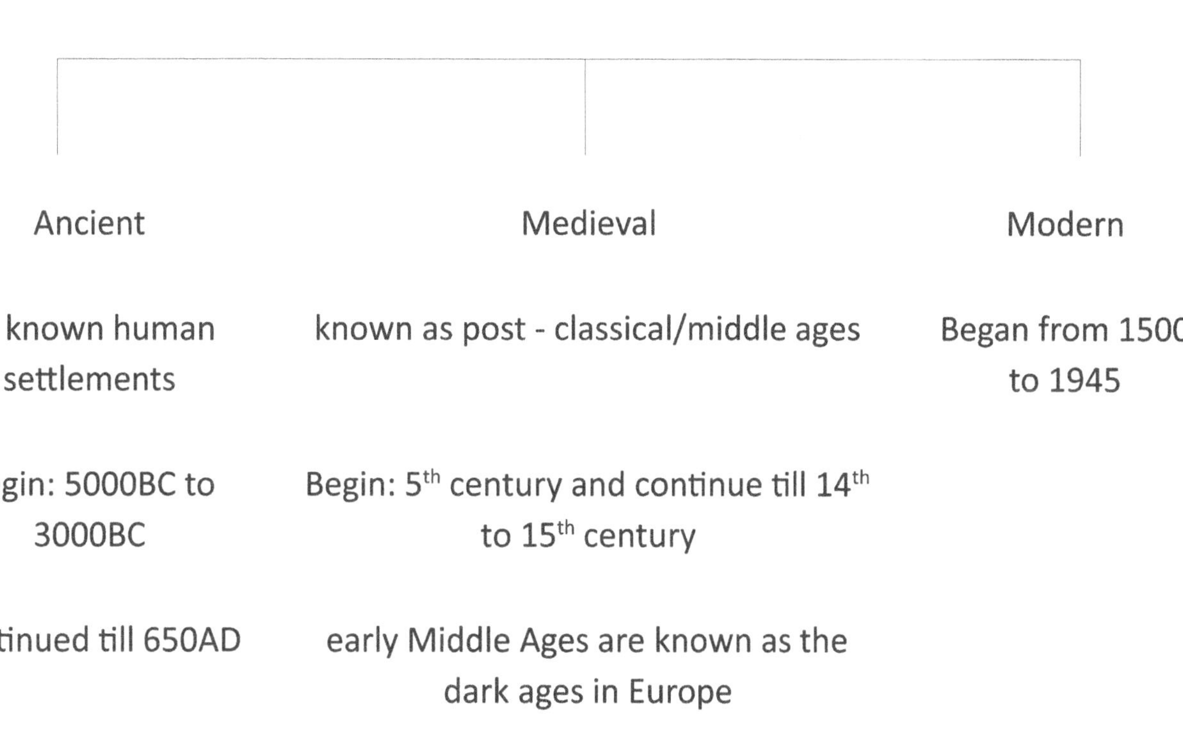

Medieval or Middle age

During 12th to 14th century

The economic prosperity of Europe increases

Increasing thinking of society

Destroyed feudalism and encouraged humanism welfare of people

[people gave kings and lords money and they offered protection]

Renaissance [Period In Europe History]

Transition from the Middle Ages to modernity

Called as scholars or scholasticism

Lead to intellectual and artistic movements for Learning wave

Called as scholars or scholasticism

Learning more than philosophy or theology

Rise in scientific thoughts

[Europe was producing new goods and was also in search of markets]

1337-1453: England and France fought 100 years war

1348: Black Death Plague disease too many lives

1453: Constantinople in the hands of Ottoman Turk Empire

In the modern period; Western Europe was in search of new trade routes

During the end of reign of 15th century: European expeditions started for new routes

1492: Columbus set out for India but reached America

1498: Vasco De Gama through Africa reached India

Led to the initiation of modern world

BEGINNING OF MODERN WORLD/ RENAISSANCE [Means RE-BIRTH and Started from Italy Florence]

- After the fall of West Roman Empire, it became part of the <u>Byzantine Empire</u>

Also known as the Eastern Roman Empire

Western Europe; In search of technology – disappeared in dark ages

RENAISSANCE played the main role in helping Europe in the Dark Ages

During 1095 to 1295 also called as Religion Wars [CRUSADES]

Christianity to Turkish Islamic followers

To Capture the holy place of "Jerusalem"

RISE IN RELIGIOUS THEORIES AND SCIENTIFIC KNOWLEDGE

1453: Ottoman Turks captured Constantinople

Resulted into the migration of Byzantine Greek Scholars to Rome

why Rome?

→venice, Florence, etc. other Italy cities not engaged in inter-city wars & not under dominance of Roman Catholic Church

Rich merchants of Italy (Rome) were ready to Patronage Greek Scholars of Byzantine

[Due to Italy was trying to find "Roman Greek Civilization"]

Rich merchants of Italy spent on

{art}

{paint

literature

{architecture}

ROMAN HUMANISM [INTELLECTUAL VERSION OF HUMANISM DERIVED FROM HUMANITAS]

Focused on human centric life

Focused on dharma instead of Karma education

RATIONAL THINKING} Replaced Theology and Superstition's

Instead of Heaven and hell Human Borrow, joy life

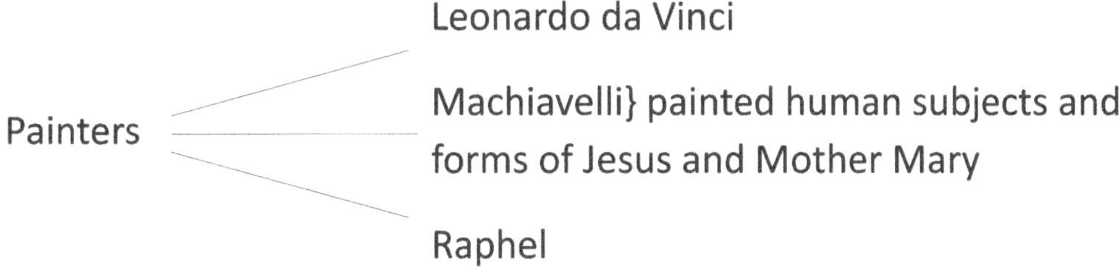

RENAISSANCE – worked on local European languages to develop

Examples:

Dante Alighieri – Authored "Divine comedy''

Machiavelli – Authored "the prince ''

Francesco Petraraca – authored "Hundred Love Sonnets ''

They got bright lightened when,

15th Century: Johannes Gutenberg (invented the printing Press) ----- education and new thinking, easy to spread

Reformation

The church was trying to maintain its dominant position in society through political powers and taxes.

1346-1353: Speed of black death plague (believed that 50% population of Europe died)

- The invention of the printing press spread secular ideas in Europe.

    - Church's authority was turning fragile.

    - Question started to raise on churches.

    - Powerful monarchs and rulers also against church centralized power in Europe.

    - Church participated in buying artifacts and luxury items.

    - The church had a luxurious lifestyle through wealth accumulation

    Priest and lower clergy: engaged in illicit affairs in church, rather than teaching and preaching ideas of religion

     In late 1300's

    - John Wycliffe of {Initiated church reforms}

- In the early 1400's

    - Jan Hus of Bohemia {Initiated church reforms}

    - Church was extorting money from the public.

    - No respect for the church.

    - Church was spelling letter of Indulgence (Sold through clergy)-who buys these letter will free from sins.

 Intiated chaos on acclaiming the bible as the light of world

[IN 1500'S Decidius Erasmus and Thomas More also thinkers also supported]

Due to the printing press, the bible was translated into local languages on a mass scale

People were now, not dependent on priests and clergy to understand these books

Between social, political and economic conditions GERMANY [new changes developed similar to religious changes]

1517: German monk MARTIN LUTHER started a campaign against the monopoly of catholic church and the pope

Believed that people who have faith in god are equal

No need for priests to explain or interpret the bible} MARTIN LUTHER

He ordered his followers to trust in the bible and god

Luther's Ideas were "popularized in Switzerland by

Ulrich Zwingli

Jean Calvin

Due to such Campaigns, Churches of Germany and Switzerland broke relations with the pope & Catholic church

 Martin Luther's campaign was supported by ------ printing press

--mouth of publicity

--merchant class

--farmers

[Some rulers of Rome Supported protestants to free authority of Catholic Church]

Europe catholic allowed Protestants to worship Church in their Comfortable way

Instead of Latin, a local language was used by sermons

Reformation Parliament

Henry vi

1589: The ruler of England (Henry vlll) called for the Reformation of Parliament & broke relations with pope Sat from 1529 to 1536

- legislation passed to Greek with rope and increase in authority of Church of England

Legislation passed to Greek with Rome an increase in Authority of church of England

After this,

Church men in Spain and Italy started simple life and Service of poor

Reformation "disassociated / Church" from defined State, Politics & Economy

-- Led to rise in secular states

-- Nationalism in Europe

CONCLUSION: The above topics affected to initiate French, American and Industrial revolutions

- legislation passed to Greek with rope and increase in authority of Church of England

American Revolution

USA; is the first County to adopt Democratic Republican System – Combines both Democratic and Republic

--- Alterations in European politics

* 1789: French Revolution

* 1798: Ireland revolt} Inspired and influenced by American Revolution

* 1830s:Latin American revolt

* 1830s: Latin American revolt

• In 20th century, decolonization moments of African Asia were captured

1492AD: discovery of America by Columbus ---- Also landed in Caribbean Islands and named it as West Indies

[Geographer Amerigo Vespussi surveyed entire the continent and named AMERICA]

• Europeans called Americans as native or red Indians

FROM 16TH CENTURY: European power started settling in America

-Portuguese established colonies in Brazil.

-England and France established colonies in USA and Canada.

-Britian (1st colony in Virginia in 1609) established 13 colonies in North America

• New Hampshire

• New york

• Pennsylvania

- Massachusetts
- Rhode Island} located on east coast and these colonies are called New England
- Connecticut
- New jersey
- Delaware
- Maryland
- North Carolina
- South Carolina
- Georgia(1732)-last colony

--Between 1775-1781:13 colonies was against British and known as "American war of Independence"

–Britian lost and ended with-1783: Paris Treaty (America declared independence).

17th Century Political setup

In Britain, American Colonies Had legislative, Executive wing elected by people

Top position: Governer / military chief appointed by Britain

Britain provides economic, political help to colonies

In 1730s distinct identity was emerged in north America

2nd and 3rd gen people played important role in socio – cultural and economic development

SOCIO – CULTURAL SETUP

AMERICAN SOCIETY WAS LIBERAL AND PROGRESSIVE

*Europe faced a problem of religious persecution

*Europe --- Protestants and Catholics lived peacefully in America

Harvard University [

Religious rivalry was absent due to inspiration from Renaissance established William and Mary college ['1693]

Harvard University [1636]

Yale University [1701]

University of Pennsylvania [1701]

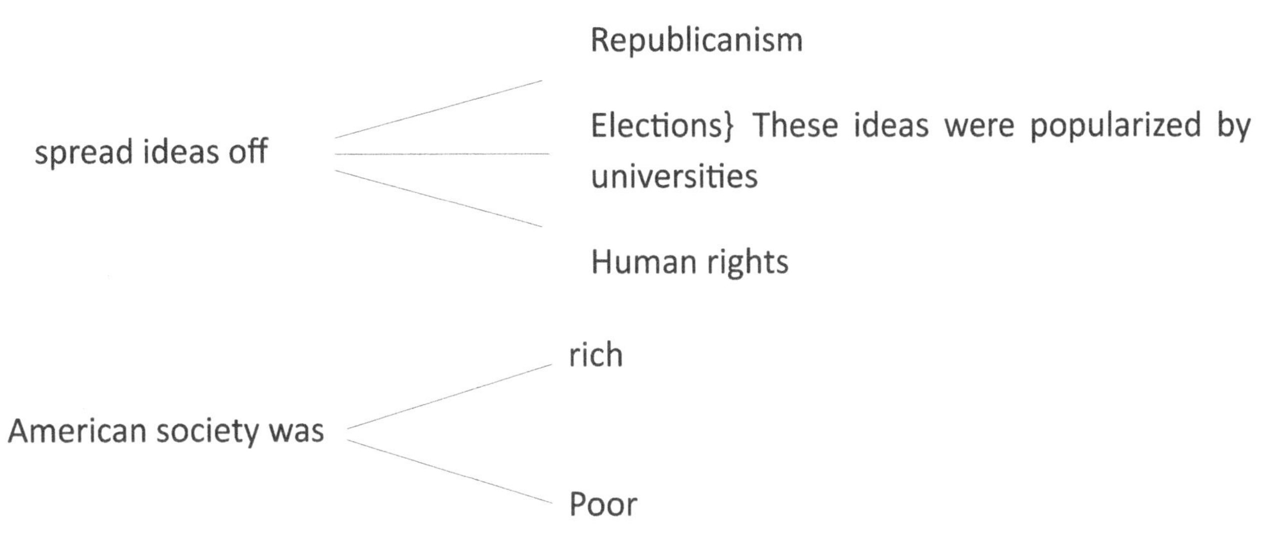

AMERICAN SOCIETY POOR

--America developed meritocracy or meritocracy OR MERITORIOUS SYSTEM

ECONOMIC SETUP

Based on capitalism and free market system

European settlers want economic progress in America

*agricultural crops – cotton

--- Tobacco

--- sugarcane

- Industries ----- ship building

Timber

Mining industries

Britain trade policies are in a way that, it benefits only Britain people not American colonies.

Britain trade policies in America

-Britain passed many acts to control American trade and economy.

- **1651Navigation act: only use of Britain ships for trade.**
- **Enumerated Commodities Act (1660): only Britain can export sugar, cotton, Indigo, Tabacco.**
- **Staple act (1663): Britain takes American goods before exporting**
- **Iron act (1750)**
- **Hat act**
- **Woollen act (controversial acts regarding trade)**

   1754: Some Intellectuals organised "Albany congress" (represented by 7 out of 13 colonies) against these policies.

   - Benjamin Franklin proposed to form "American" but not accepted

American union was not accepted because they were facing

* French aggression

French were settled in North American on the west of Mississippi River

[French people trying to capture England's colonies]

The Britain didn't took any action to threats which may result in weaken of Britain position

1754 to 1763: Seven Years war between French and British

Britain won

- *also it led to the plantation of American revolution

7 years war and its aftermath

- This war was also fought in America and India ----- To secure colonial possessions

British colonies extended till the Appalachian Mountains in the West

France control beyond Appalachian Mountains

France controlled Louisiana to Great Lakes region in America

1763: Seven Years War ended

* Britian won

* France surrendered Britain colonies that were controlled

* Pushed Britain into debt

* Financial crisis in Britain ---- to recover debt, new taxes were introduced in colonies

Britain introduces unpopular legislation and taxes such as

- Sugar act 1764: Britain can only export sugar to colonists
- Quartering act 1764: Britain soldiers in America should take care of their expenses by America
- Stamp act 1765: tax on legal documents

Chaos resulted in America due to this acts

[But Britain thinks it was valid because tax was used for colonies development]

 --America thinks tax authority would be on locals but not on Britain Parliament

Raise of famous slogan

NO TAXATION WITHOUT REPRESENTATION

- No American in Britain Parliament so British did not have the authority to impose tax
- Samuel Adams set sons of Liberty ---- boycott of Britain goods and trade
- Committee of correspondence set up to popularize the idea of Independence

1765: Declaratory actually by Britain (sole power to make laws)

1767: Townshend actually (Tax on tea, paper, glass, land, paint)

Townshend actually was opposed and Boston massacre took place

- led to more pressure on Britain

- Britain PM Lord North took down new taxes except tea tax(It was an important source of revenue for Britain)

"Without American permission No Tax or No Act can be introduced on them"

- **Boston Tea party: under the leadership of Samuel Adams, Tea from ships are thrown into the sea.**

1774: Intolerance act by Britain

* Ban of political me

* Closed Boston Port to find tea party culprits

1774: first Continental Congress – Reaction to Britain

- Boycott Britain goods
- Use of domestic goods

Thomas Paine wrote *the pamphlet*: 1775 to 1776

[Merits of separation of America from Britain's]

1776: second Continental Congress [Adopted declaration of independence pledge]

British King, GeorgeIII declared war on American colonies

1776-81: American war of independence

Britain led by Lord Cornwallis

-America led by George Washington.

-Americans support from Spain and France.

- 1781: With surrender of Cornwallis in Yorktown, war ended.
- 1783: Treaty of Paris- Britain recognized as American independence.

- 1787: Organized Constitutional convention at Philadelphia. Drafted constitution

- Significance:

  -Free nation

  -Fundamental rights

- 1787: Organized Constitutional convention at Philadelphia. Drafted constitution

American Civil War / Unstable War

- Civil war- was fought between different people living in same country

    Main motive of civil war:

    -To control any region of county.

    Revolt against government policies.

    American civil war (1862-1865)
- Fought between "Union" "(the north)" and "(confederacy")" "(the south)"
- South USA wants to establish as a separate confederacy from USA

Reasons for civil war:

-Slavery system of America

-Inequalities between North and South America

19th century: American Witnessed Industrial Revolution

- effects only in North America

No positive impacts in South America --- people used as slaves and produced crops like cotton and tobacco

During this reign America in West was expanding and people supported slavery in Westside

[Slavery system opposed by North and supported by South]

1830: Anti slavery movements

[Not prevalent in South American region]

1854: act passed by Southern USA

[Legalized slavery]

Chaos between pro slavery and slavery abolitionists groups – called BLEEDING KANSANS

- Republican party formed
- Abraham Lincoln made president of USA
- Abolition of slavery
- Under Lincoln, South USA (7 states) was separated and formed "confederates of America" and American union divided
- Result into Civil war.
- Civil war Began
- COA attacked Fort Sumter in Charleston
- 13th April 1862, COA captured Fort Sumter.
- Arkansas, tennessee, North Carolina, virgina (joined COA).

Civil bar Battles

1st battle of bull run (21st July 1861)

- Confederates lead by Jackson
- Union army lost
- George B Mccellan made new leader of union army.

2nd Battle of Bull Run [29th August 1862]

*Union Army Lost

Battle of Maryland

Confederates defeated

Union army won

Battle of Sharpsburg

Bloodiest day in American history

   - Lincoln issued emancipation proclamation

- Freed slavery and join them in army

- Union army strengthened

- SOUTH USA economy downfall

Ending of civil war

- Union army under ULYSSESS S.Grant defeated Confederates

- On 9th april, Confederates surrendered by ending war in 1865

• Civil war was officially ended on 26th April 1865

French Revolution

Causes

- Social causes

- -French society was divided into :   1st estate – FOR CLERGY

  2nd estate – NOBILITY

  3rd estate – COMMONS

-Majority represent 3rd estate (By paying higher taxes and social, political rights)

Economic causes

- 1st and 2nd estates were exempted from tax
- More burden on 3rd estates
- Political causes

King Louis XVI (weak monarch)

- Neglected poor masses were rising tensions/angry.
- Intellectual causes

- French thinkers rejected divine right theory (18th century)
- Thinkers promoted doctrine of equality
- Rousseau(thinker)- rejected absolute monarchy
- Also promoted people's sovereignity.

COURSE OF REVOLT

France economy was down-teared and in 1786, Louis XVI Controller general of Charles Alexander proposed financial reform package

- Universal land tax was also included

1789: summoning of Estates General by Louis XVI to discuss financial reform package

General Assembly of France

*Every estate has one vote

* 3rd state demanded head by vote --- want political change and to remove power of 1st and 2nd estate

On 17 June, third estates themselves adopted title National Assembly

- Louis XVI stops 3rd state entry to Palace of Versailles

Third estate met at tennis court and want to draft new constitution

[Tension emerges and on 14th of July, there was an attack on Bastille]

Through assembly – "Declaration of the rights of man and citizen passed"

-It was death certificate of ancient feudal order.

- **1791: Drafted new constitution**
  - **Gave dominance to middle classes**

    Every citizen have civil rights but voting rights to fewer (only who have property or paid fixed tax to government)
  - **France transformed from "Absolute to Constitutional monarchy"**

    Challenges for new Assembly
  - **Non monarchy and monarchs rivalry**
  - **1st and 2nd estates lost privileges and made allegations on government**
- **Austria and Prussia alliances to bring monarchy in France**
- **New government "National convention" was formed and is in power between (1792-1795: violet phase of revolution)**

- **This government was dominant through Radicals**
- **Radicals want Republicity in France**
- **After Louis death France declared Republic**
- **Have two sections**
- **Maximiliem de Robespierre – save economy from tension**

1795: drafted new constitution by National Convention

- 5 members for France administration

- No any men can exploit power

- Directors were corrupt and collapsed

Napoleon crushed France's internal disturbance

1799: directors replaced by French consulate

--Three members in consulate

-- Dictatorship started by Napoleon

1804: Napoleon declared himself as Emperor and people accepted it

- Which ended French revolution
- Again France entered monarchy

Significance of revolution

Emergence of new ideas such as liberalism democracy and enlightenment

Ideas spread to Europe

ended feudalism

Industrial Revolution

- Refers to change in production system

[Coal and steam engine are used for production]

--It was first begin in Britain during 1750 to 1760s

[It's first began in Britain because its favorable geographical conditions, commodity sources, colonial trade and economic scientific methods agricultural reform society and policies]

Causes for revolution or change

Britain's geography and resources

Surrounded by water and free from attacks

Favorable coastline for sea ports

Warm Gulf currents make open ports for years

Has abundant coal and iron resources

To protect ports Britain developed Navy Army

Due to Britain's strong Naval Army, Napoleon was failed to defeat Britain Navy

A. Agricultural reforms in Britain

Rapid agricultural growth in 16th and 17th century

   Fencing of agricultural land

   Increased farm size

Crop rotation techniques

Sowing seeds through drill

Use of fertilizers and irrigation system

B. Scientific discoveries

Invention of flying shuttle by John Kay in 1733 [textile industry]

Spinning jenny by James Hargreaves in 1764 AD

Waterframe by Richard Arkwright ------- founder of textile industry

James Watt invented steam engine in 1769

James Stevenson invented railway steam engine in 1814 AD

[First train was from Liverpool to Manchester in 1830]

C. Economy and banking

Profitable economy through trade during 17th and 18th century

Led to surplus capital and invested in industries

Led to emergence of joint stock companies ------- Established by one or more persons it finances projects that are too expensive for govt too

Effects on economy

Progressive growth

Wide use of logistics for wider reach of goods

Let to development of industrial capitalism

Establishing of joint stock trading companies

Only domestic industries fell backward

Engineering, company law, economics, management are newly added in universities for education

New phenomena of recession and economic boom ----- Impacted industry and trade

Political effects

Public demanded freedom and fundamental rights

Feudalism and aristocracy are replaced by liberal political thoughts ----- Which led to emergence of capitalist and middle class in Europe

Workers condition was getting degraded which led to formation of trade unions---- It was recognized by Britain in 1825

Conflicts between capitalist and worker class which led to rise of socialism

Led by Robert owen

Saint Simon} Industrial intellectual class

Louis Blanc

Fried Rich Angels

Effects on society and culture

Three classes emerged

- Capitalist [Controls economy and national politics]
- Middle class [Doctors, engineers, managers, agents, scientist, lawyers, teachers]
- Workers and peasants

--Workers were survived in inhumane condition

--Led to both of trade union movements

--Based on financial status, social relations were formed

Encouraged ——— CONSUMERISM [To protect interests of consumers]

MATERIALISM [Importance on stuff]

Led to urbanization

Down fall off society standards due to rise in crime rate

19th century industrialization was witnessed in

America

France

Japan

Italy

Germany

Imperialism and Colonialism

Started from Europe

Imperialism means
- Power projection
- economy and political domination

Colonialism means
- Physical takeover of a nation's resources
- Permanent settlement of people

1500AD: age of modern colonialism starts

[start's, when sea route is discovered between US and Africa]

Portugal, Spain, France, Dutch Republic, England established in other countries through 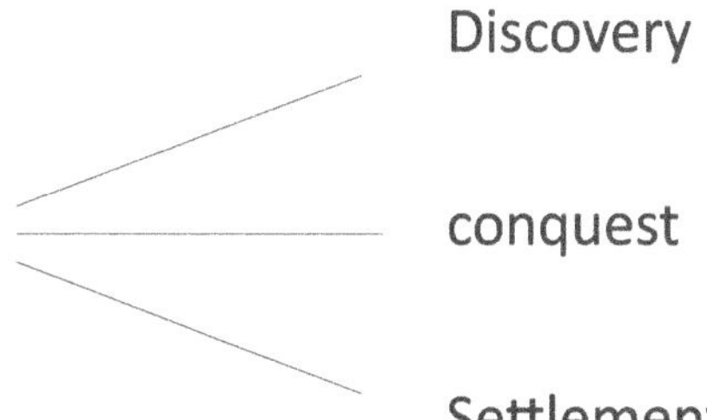
- Discovery
- conquest
- Settlement

Settlement

- **Age of Imperialism (1870- 1914)**
  - Old Imperialism Era (between 16th – 19th century)
  - European set trading posts in Africa, Asia and Middle East during New Imperialism in 1870's.

- Economic reasons
  - Industrialized nations extension for excess product.
  - Colonies provided labours and coaling stations to Europe navies.
- Colonialism
  - Humanitarian goals

    1890: Whitemans Burden mission by Rudyard Kipling

    -Missionaries supported it for Christianity propagation in Asia and Africa

    -Social Darwinism boasted colonialism

    Social Darwinism
  - 1859: "on the origin of species" by Charles Darwin

    -Theory of "Survival of fittest"
  - Herbert Spencer; 1st person to apply. Darwin's theory on Human societies and nation
  - -Colonialism also boasted by Western technology
- Quinine invention to cure tropical Diseases
- Steamboat and telegraph mobilized west
- Rapid fire gun for military advantage

--Imperialism created amid tension between Morocco, France, Germany and Ottoman Empire which, result into World war.

Unification of Germany

19th century: Germany emerged as organized nation

Prior to 19th century, Germany was divided into 300 kingdoms

Background

Most kingdoms were part of Roman Empire

1803 to 1815: Napoleanic Wars were fought by Napoleon and major portion of Europe is annexed

Built Rhine Federation of 39 German states for effective rule

[Established German Parliament or diet for 39 states]

--Eliminated trade barriers

-- promoted free trade

--German nationalism also developed

1813: Battle of Leipzig with Britain} Ended Napoleon rule

1815: Battle of Waterloo with Russia}

1815: Vienna Congress headed by Britain, Austria, Prussia, Russia

[39 boundaries are not subjected to change]

Austria was made as Rhine Federation leader

Later changed into German confederation

BURSCHENSCHAFT (Student organization network)

For strengthening pan German hood

Want to popular United Republican idea

Fire of unification was rising

Austria and Prussia fighting for German leadership

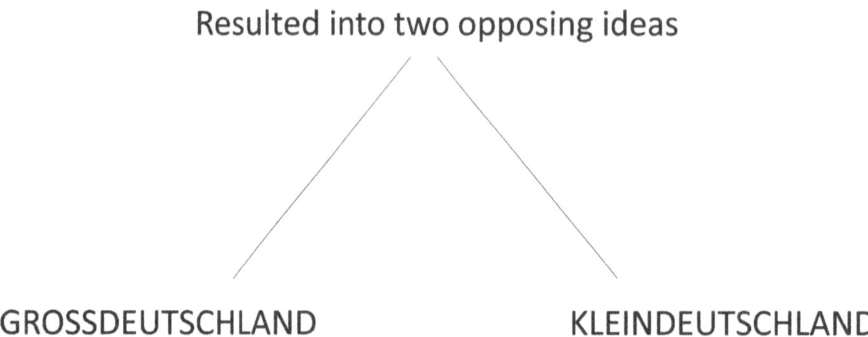

[Austria included] [Austria not included and favored by Prussia]

Zolleverein or economic integration

1818: Prussia remote trade tariffs due to trade hamper

1836: Zolleverein led by Prussia was coalition of twenty five German states

Revolutions of 1848

Revolutionaries demanded Democratic government and civil rights

[Decided to build <u>parliament in Frankfurt a</u> symbol of unification]

Given responsibility of new constitution

Failed to unify Germany

Limited King Power in proposal of new constitution

 Austria threatened Prussia for war not to bring changes in 39 states

1862: <u>ottoman Bismarck</u> appointed as PM of Prussia

[Main architect to unify Germany]

<u>Bismarck and blood and iron policy</u>

Represented Prussia in Russia and France

Wanted to unite all states under Prussia

Prussian Reichstag [parliament]

Liberals   Socialist   conservative

[Supported Democracy] [Supported Worker's rights] [Supported King or monarchy]

* Bismarck wanted people to turn towards monarchy and took many steps to satisfy different nations

Started army modernizations

Bismarck policies were also known as <u>realpolitik or osteopolitik</u>

Decisions were based on interest and real circumstances not on ethics and ideology

<u>War and diplomacy</u>

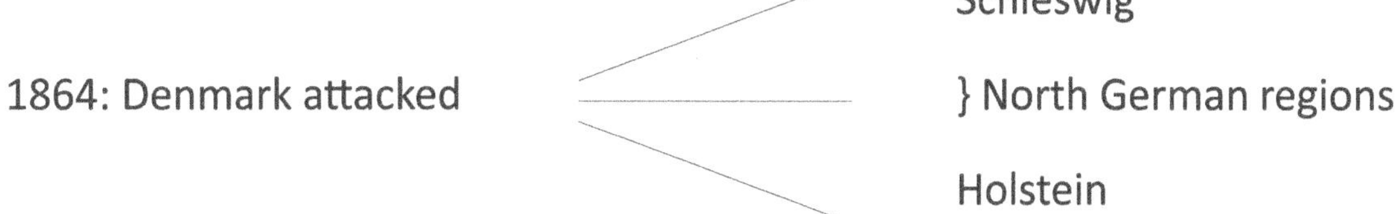

1864: Denmark attacked

Prussia and Austria was united for war as Denmark was common in enemy and won with Denmark

Received Schleswig Received Holstein

Bismarck forcing Holstein people against Austria

1866: Australia declared war on Prussia

In 1863, Prussia helped Russia in Poland revolt

Made Russia as an ally by Bismarck

Made agreement with Napoleon III in France --- To stay neutral in future Austro Prussian War and Russia handed some regions to France

23rd August, 1866: treaty of Prague

Dissolved 1815 Vienna Agreement

Made 21 states of Confederation

Bismarck denied regions of France, he want to fight with France

[Through EMS Telegram System, France got hurt their emotions and declared war on Prussia]

1870: Franco- Prussian War

All German states united

Prussia on war

King Frederick William was the 1st emperor of United Germany and Bismarck as 1st chancellor

[Through blood and iron policy of 1864 to 1871, Germany was unified]

Conclusion

Germany as emergence of powerful state in Europe

Germany as superpower joined in list of Britain, France and Russia

Participation of Germany in colonial competition

Unification of Italy (19th century)

- **It was during reign of nationalism and emerging new nations/states**
  - **It was social and political movement**
  - **Single states by consolidation Kingdoms**
    - -- Unification also known as "Risorgimento" (Itatian language aimed to revive ancient Roman Empire of Italy).
- **Causes for unification**
  - **Italy is surrounded by water from 3 sides.**
  - **North Italy has Alps mountain.**
  - **Those make Italy a closed geographical unit.**

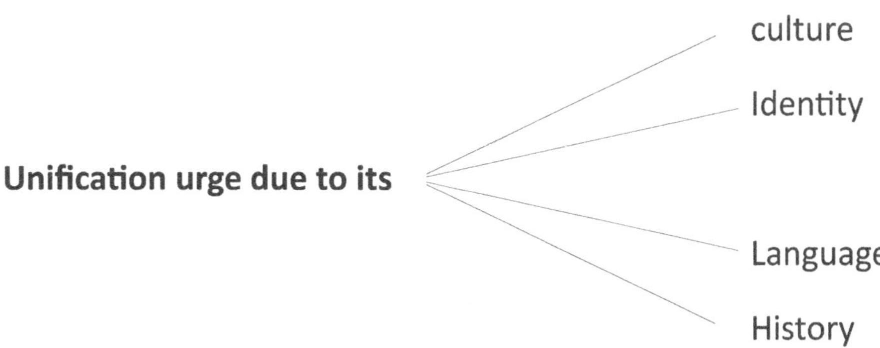

- **1804: Napolean became France and Italy emperor by making small regions of Italy included in France.**
  - **Promoted trade**
  - **Low code**
  - **Ended Feudal system**
  - **Promoted Nationalism and Republicanism in Italy.**

After Napoleon's defeat, Vienna Congress came to maintain power

--Restored earlier boundaries of Italy

--Not made Italian states independent

 Distributed Italian kingdoms

Venice and Lombardy [Northern Italy]--- under Habsburg Empire of Austria

Parma, Moderna and Tuscany --- Under indirect rule of Austria

Naples and Sicily [Southern Italy]--- Under Bourbon Empire of France

Papal states [Capital Rome]---- Under direct control of pope---- Important religious figure of Catholic Christianity

Piedmont and Sardinia are independent

The division by Vienna Congress led the urge of nationalism in Italy

Revolutionary Diplomacy Two methods to unify Italy

[By Mazzini and Garibaldi] [By count Cavour]

Revolutionary methods of Mazzini and Garibaldi

- **Secret societies (carbonari) formed to overthrow government from Italy.**

    Initiated uprisings (1820, 1831, 1848)—Famous uprisings, but suppressed.

    - **1831: Giuseppe Mazzini (heart of Italian unification) formed his revolutionary society called "Young Italy"**

    -wants to transform as Democratic Republic Nation.

- He succeeded in capturing Rome in 1848, but taken back by Napolean -- established Republic of Rome

- He was deported to America and death in 1872.

- **Diplomatic methods of count cavour (Brain of Italian unification)**
    - **Cavour was PM of Piedmont and sardinia under Italian kingdom of Victor Immanuel**
        - **Started newspaper Risorgimento**
        - **wanted to unite Italy under piedmont and Sardinia leadership.**

- **Cavour adopted**
- **Wanted Italy to take Sardinia (so internal development of Sardinia is necessary)as Ideal.**
- **Gave citizens rights and press freedom, even though Sardinia was monarchy.**
  - **1853-56: Cavour used his 1st diplomatic skill during Crimean war [Russian Empire VS Ottoman Empire, France, Britain, Italy (later added)].**
  - **- Defeated Russia**
  - **- Peace conference in Paris.**
  - **Cavour raised issue of suppression of Northern Italy by Austria and gained sympathy of Britain and France.**
  - **France supported Sardinia by opposing Austria.**
  - ***Napolean III**
  - **--- Cavour established matrimonial relations**
  - **--Gave Savory and Nice (on France and Sardinia Border) to France.**
  - **Important phases to unity Italy**
- **Phase 1: 1858-59**

Nothern Itlay kingdoms against Australian rules, but Austria declared war on Sardinia.

-France help led to freedom Lambardy, but failed in venice.

-Lombardy included in Sardinia Kingdom.

Phase 2: 1860

Purma, Moderna and Tuscany also raised their voice against Austria

*Austria wants to suppress, but Cavour was offended

* kingdom's wanted Plebiscite--- which means public decision

People wanted to join Sardinia

Those regions joined in parts of Piedmont and Sardinia

Except Venice and Rome all parts were engaged

Southern Italy ———————— NAPLES} UNDER INDIRECT RULE OF FRANCE

SICILY

1860: GARIBALDI liberates them --- chosen by Cavour

He wants Republican in south

Rejected South to include in Nort

Napoleon III permitted Cavour to attack Naples and Sicily to freed from rebellion

Cavour signed deal with Garibaldi

Garibaldi agreed to unite them in nor

 Only Venice and Rome left

Phase 3: 1866,1876

--Cavour died in 1862 and unification responsibility was on shoulders of Victor Immanuel. II

- Victor sings a secret agreement with Prussia.

•Sardinia supports Prussia.

•Prussia should handle venice to Sardinia.

•1866: Austro-Prussian war

-Prussia won

-Sardinia government venice (According to agreement).

-Only Rome left.

- **1871: Franco- Prussian war**
  - **Nepolean called army from Rome.**
  - **Victor capture by advantage of Rom.**
  - **Only Vatican City (small part) was under pole.**
  - **unification done.**
  - **Victor Immanuel II was Emperor.**

World War - 1

Entire world divided into allied powers and central powers

RUSSIA, FRANCE, BRITIAN and USA -- ALLIED POWERS

AUSTRO-HUNGARIAN EMPIRE, GERMANY AND OTTOMAN EMPIRE---- CENTRAL POWERS

Causes

Militarism (ARMS-RACE) – supported by Britain U S A and Germany

Alliance system – 1882: Triple alliance: Germany Italy Austro-Hungarian Empire

1904: Entente Cordiale Alliance by France and Britain

Imperialism --- colonial expansion race

Nationalism

Russia and Ottoman Empire were in conflict of controlling Strait of Dardanelles

Connects Aegean sea and sea of Marmar

Its gateway to Mediterranean sea via Black sea

- Immediate cause

- Assasination of Austro- Hungarian prince Archduke Franz Ferdinand and his wife on 28th June, 1914

- By Gavrilo princep (belong to Serbia)

- **Reasons for Escalation of war**

    --Alliance system -1984: Alliance between France and Russia sealed Europe.

    --Naval Race between Germany and Britain – Every country wants to show their Supremacy.

    --Desire for Economic mastery- Blamed Capitalist system.

Russian Revolution (1917)

Most explosive political events of 20th country

-Ended Roman Dynasty rule.

-Ended Imperial rules.

-Bolsheviks gained power.

- **Background**
  - **During that region, most countries followed French Republic or Britain constitutional monarch.**

    -Russia still ruled by Czars (Russian Emperors)
- **1861:Serfdom was abolished**

  -Peasants worked for landlords.

  -peasants didn't improve.
- **Russian Industrialisation started in later half of 19th century.**

  -workers condition was horrible

  - Czar NicholasII believed in Divine rights of kings and protected absolutism.

Prohibited Political parties by order of Government

[Internal passport system to restrict people's movement]

Growth of revolutionary movements

19th century: Going to the people was rising agitation

(Intellectuals preach ideas to peasants)

1883: Russian Social Democratic Party was formed under George Plekhanove

1898: changes into Russian Social Democratic labour Party

Mensheviks – minority In elections

Bolsheviks – majority in elections

Led by Vladimir Ilyich Ulyanov

There was also socialist revolutionary party engaged in rising peasantry demand

1905: Prelude to Revolution

Russia defeated by Japan in (1904 to 05) – 1st time European was defeated by Asian

9th Jan, 1905: Rebellion against autocracy and "Bloody Sunday" (led by Father Gapon) event.

***Bloody Sunday:**

-People marched to petition for Tsar Nicholas.

-People dead in firing.

-Led to strikes and chaos.

• Tsar Nicholas. To leave the rebellions, gives a manifesto(speech, press and association granted freedom)

and talked about election legislature (Duma).

--Russia also become constitutional monarch.

--Duma:

First National representative institution in Russia

-less power.

Legal powers and parties emerged.

World war 1 Russian Empire

- **Russian faced biggest casualties**

- **Nicholas under Alexandra, his wife [she fires election officials in absence of Czars (Who went to war)].**

Less availability of bread

Army loss

Lenin proposed two ideas for successful revolution

- People should be ready to lose their lives

- Current government should be in crisis

LEADS TO FEBRUARY REVOLUTION

February Revolution

Working class women for bread and later joined by soldiers

8th March 1970: It started and also enters into St Petersburg and Moscow

[It was called as February Revolution due to use of Julian calendar in Russia]

Revolution according to calendar: 23rd February, 1918

March 12th: Provisional government by Duma and Romanov Dynasty rule ended

Led by Alexander Kerensky

October or Bolshevik Revolution

Provincial government
- Land to the tiller
- Industry control} Kerensky Govt. didn't accept these four demands and people lost their support
- Peace

Under Lenin leadership,

Bolsheviks want to curb war and transfer the land to peasants

Slogan --- ALL POWER TO THE SOVIETS

Lenin depicted Russian nation as prison of nations and declared that no democracy can be established

Voice on self determination and rights

7th November, 1917: Kerensky government collapsed

Bolsheviks also occupied government property

All Russian Congress meeting of Soviets

Formation of new government

It was peaceful revolution

Civil war in Russia between Czar Officer's organized armed Rebellion against Soviet troops

- **Consequences of Revolution**

  -Abolished autocracy(ended Czar rule).

  -Destroyed powers of Church.

  -Union of Soviet Socialist Republic Emerged (USSR).

  Abolished private property

  -Economic planning was initiated

Rise of Hitler

- **Post world war 1 — Germany**

Germany VS England, Franch, Russia

--Germany also captured France and Belgium.

--1918, Germany defeated.

- **Led to Germany Revolution**

-William Kaiser III (runs from Germany)

-Monarchy comes to end.

- **National Assembly met at Weimar and forms democratic constitution.**

-Germanys new government is called Weimar Republic.

-Germany singed Treaty of Versailles.

***Treaty of Versailles: 1919**

-Humiliating treaty to Germans .

-Germany was war Guilt cause.

-Germany has to pay 33B$ to allied nations.

-Germany army and Navy was limited.

Hitler and Nazi party

1913: Hitler came to Germany, served the army in World War I

1919: Hitler joined German workers party and later, he became its leader

1920: It changed to national socialist German workers party or Nazi Party

Conservative Frustrated soldiers

Monarchists

Helpless workers Troubled businessmen

Nazi party

Anti Jewish Anti communist Anti catholic

MEIN KAMPF – Hitler's autobiography [Consisting of racist thoughts and German plans]

1928: Hitler got only 2% of votes

(During the great economic depression, Hitler became famous through his propaganda)

1930: Nazi's and communist's got good votes in elections but not an majority to form government

Hitler participated in president elections

Hitler's opposition were Ernst Thalman and Paul Von Hidenburg

Paul got president and Hitler on 2nd place

Nazi party with 37% of seats in Legislature

1933: Hidenburg and Chancellor Papen, were forced to sign a deal with Hitler

- Hitler made as Germany Chancellor on January 30th, 1933

Hitler becomes dictator

Hitler conducted general elections to occupy Cabinet Post

Used state machinery

Earlier got 3 seats out of 11

He posted Nazis everywhere

Political meeting of Communist's and socialist's were disrupted

Hitler passed enabling law on 23rd March, 1933 and passed in Reichstag.

-Government can pass any law without taking approval from Reichstag.

--Alliance laws should be drafted through chancellor.

•Hitler can work as dictator for 4 years.

How Hitler turns Germany into Nazi/Fascist/Totalitarian state?

•Features of Nazi Totalitarian state.

--Hitler follows Gleichschaltung policy (A forcible coordination).

- It controls more citizens aspect.

--All other political parties were banned.

- Jews and Nazi enemies were removed from civil services.

- Abolished trade unions [Instead of this, German labour front (All workers should take membership)].

- **All boys of age 14,should join "Hitler youth organization". All girls should join "League of German Maidens".**

- **Dr.Joseph Goebbles – control all types of information and media.**

- **10th May, 1933: National Book Burning day.**

  - **To burn books of socialist, Jews and suspect writers.**

  - **Germany was made as police state.**

Every wrong incident was blamed on Jews

People who were revolting against government are sent to concentration camps

Hitler's Economic Policy

To eliminate unemployment

Autarky policy--- Boost exports and reduce imports

Introduced 4 year plan in industries, about what to produce

Big projects on public works

Slum clearance

Land drainage

Motorway building

52% government spends on military budget

Hitler's religious policy

Roman Catholics and Protestants were dominant sects of Germany

1933: Concordat agreement with Pope

--[Hitler promised not to interfere with Catholics]

--[Hitler broke it and dissolved Catholic Youth League]

1937: Catholics are against Nazi

Majority of Germans were Protestants

Hitler wanted to organize them in Reich Church

Nazis proved them intolerance

Hitler's Foreign Policy

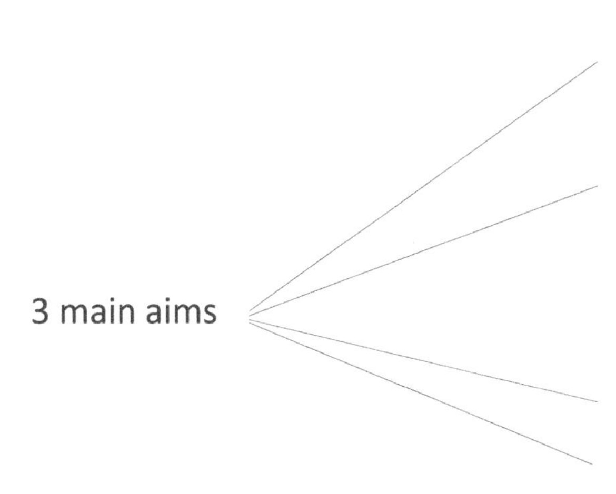

3 main aims

To destroy treaty of versailles

German speaking people in one nation – German people in Austria,Czech,Poland want to unite them

Living space for Germans called Lebensraum

He want to make GROSSDEUTSCHLAND

For this he, wanted to expand to Poland[east] and Russia[west]

Signed non- aggression pact with Poland in 1934, which ended diplomatic isolation of Germany

June, 1936: Spanish Civil War started

--Hitler helps Spain

-- Italy dictator Mussolini also helps Spain

Led to emergence of Rome Berlin Axis Alliance

1938 and 39: Hitler annexed Austria and Czechoslovakia (Britain and France were neutral due to policy of appeasement)

•1939: Hitler launched attack on Poland

-To be on safe side, he signed a non aggression pact with USSR in March 1939.

•Britain and France declared war against Germany.

°Further lead to world war 2.

Mussolini and The rise of Fascism

- **During this reign, Europe was getting attached to strong leadership.**
- **-Fascism was rising**

1919: 1st time used by Mussolini to describe his political movement.

Common features of Fascism

- **Fascist regimes, strong centralized state and establish of national government.**
- **Individual should serve state**

  • **Rule by Dictator:**

  -Fascist state are run by single dictator.

  •**Corporation:**

  -For Capitalisms, Fascists control

  -Union, sticks are illegal.

  •**Extreme nationalism:**

  -Fascist state relies on national myth.

  - Unify dominant groups in country.

  •**Militiarism and Imperialism.**

  Mussolini's Rise to power

  •**He was finding a way to unify Italy.**

  •**1918:He gave speeches on dictatorship.**

  •**1919: Mussolini organised his Fascist movement in Milan, Italy.**

-Socialists and communists were thrown out from local government

•Due to communist revolution in Russia, anti-communist business people supported fascist movement.

•1921: National Fascist party formed

Oct 29, 1922: Mussolini –Youngest PM of Italy.

-He gave speech to surrender government or his people will capture the government.

•Fascist states

Fascist party got 66% total votes in the election of 1924.

- Mussolini closes opposition newspapers
- Bans public protest meetings
- Other political parties declared illegal
- Labour Union and strikes are illegal

Established organization of vigilance and repression of anti-fascism --- Political police force

Established Fascist Grand council

1925: adopts a title DUCE (THE LEADER)

1929: Signed a treaty with church and made Catholicism as state religion

[Mussolini under Hitler's influence banned Jews from some organizations]

Mussolini's foreign policy

1935: invasion of Ethiopia

1939: signed pact of steel with Hitler – Help each other during war

--[Sent 2,00,000 soldiers for accompanying in Soviet invasion for Hitler]

1943: British and American allies defeated Italy and occupied Sicily

--Mussolini got arrest order from Victor Emmanuel

--Mussolini runs to Germany

Mussolini returns in Milan establishes fastest regime

It's controlled by Germans

Mussolini was captured by anti-fascist fighters

April 28th, 1943: Mussolini was shot

World War - 2

Immediate flashpoint

31st August, 1939: West Upper Silesia region

Nazis seized Gleiwitz radio station

Broadcasts Anti-German message

It was designed to justify Poland invasion

--Germany invades which Poland on 1st September, 1939

--Britain and France attacks Germany on 3rd September, 1939

Leads to global war or World War Two

Story of war

Germany, Italy, Japan and other small countries created Axis Fund against Britain

Early 1941: They led their dominance in Europe, North and East Africa

22nd June, 1941: Germany invaded Soviet and started eastern front

Japan attacked pearl harbour

[Soviet invasion and Pearl Harbour incident led to America enter in war]

2nd February, 1943: Soviets defeated Germans

--Led to downfall of Axis powers

-- Allied powers occupied -- German occupied France and Italy

--Japan also forced to retreat in Pacific

Assassination of Mussolini and suicide of Hitler in 1945 led to surrender of Germany

Japan was not ready to give up

America wages nuclear attacks on Japan

Japan also surrendered on 2nd September, 1945

War led to Inevitable

• Treaty of Versailles:

28th June, 1919: Versailles

• Big 4 victor Nations of world war 1- USA , UK, France and Italy.

•Blamed Germany

 *Germany:

- Harsh punish/ demand by France

*France:

-Rhineland was demilitarised.

-Demanded paid off in 2010.

-Germany print more money, to pay debt and it led to hyper infection.

- Prohibited Austro-German unification.

———————————————————————————

Great Depression of 1929(Due to treaty of Versailles)

- Stock market crash
- Unemployment
- Originated in USA, but had impact in Germany
- Industries collapsed (As loans were given under dowes plan of 1924)
- Treatment of Germany, Italy and Japan by victors and economic crises led to worldwar 2.
- Due to Rise of Fascism and Nazism

Rise of Fascism and Nazis

Totalitarianism and dictatorship was on rise

Italy is called Fasivad

Germany is called Nazivad

Due to economic crisis and political unrest, Mussolini established 1st fascist dictatorship

(Gave rise to radical elements in Japan)

1919: League of Nations was formed but failed to establish rule of law

1941: Germany invaded Soviet and entered in World War II

Decolonization

Modern colonialism was initiated by Western European nations in 15th century AD

State of colonization

15th century: Due to Renaissance, discovery of new sea routes and navies became began among Europeans

15th century: Spain and Portugal

16th century: Britain, France and Dutch} Main colonizers

20th century: Germany, Russia, Japan

Major colonies between World War I and World War II

In World War one, after defeat of Germany and Ottoman Empire, their colonies are under League of Nations

Britain major colonies: India, Australia and Kenya

France colonies: Algeria and Vietnam

Russian colonies: Kazakhstan, Uzbekistan

Portugal colonies: Angola, Mozambique

Spain colonies: Equatorial Guinea

During World War II, Japan's territorial expansion at its peak

(Vietnam, Indonesia, Malaipeninsula, Singapore Myanmar dominated by Japan)

USA was again colonized

Philippines and Samoa were it's colonies} To maintain hegemony in Pacific Ocean

Causes of Decolonization

Growing nationalism

During World War I, Britain promised self rule for some colonies of India but later refused

[From World War I, axis powers suppressed allied powers]

1941: Atlantic Charter by USA and Britain to get favor of colonies

There was no place for territorial expansion of the World War II

Due to external pressure: USA and USSR were in favor of decolonization

Decolonization of Africa

- **Before world war 2, Liberia, Egypt and Ethiopia were only independent countries.**
- **In Britain colonies, decolonization was based on "Population of white settlers".**
  - **1956: Suez war with Egypt, Britain understood wind of change**
- **Population of whitesettlers were small in west Africa regions, so they got early independence.**
  - **1980: Zimbabwe was the last country to get independence from Britain.**
  - **Portugal decided to independent Mozambique and Angola to avoid humanities from Soviet war (1975)**

    France decolonization of Africa
  - **Brazzaville declaration (1944)**
- **It will not allow independence to any of its colonies.**
  - **1954: After Vietnam war, France geo- political become weak.**
- **Tunisa, Morocco, Madagascar and Algeria got freedom.**

    By global anti- colonial wave, Spain decolonization Equatorial Guinea and Somalia by Italy freed.

Cold war

1945: Allied forces　　　　defeated　　　　Axis powers

USA, Britain, France, Soviet　　　　Germany, Italy and Japan

The end of World War II was beginning of Cold War

1945: Allied forces met warmly after defeating Nazis near Elbe River

It led to rivalry among them called cold war

What is the Cold War

US and Soviets become world's greatest power

[Rivalry between them led to Cold War]

[It was an ideological battle between communism and capitalism]

US was angry with USSR by signing non-aggression pact with Germany in 1939 by Joseph Stalin

Allies were blamed by Stalin about invasion on German occupied Europe

America used atom bombs in World WarII to stop Soviet from taking political and military gains in Asia

Emergence of two power blocks

Alliance's system led by two superpowers, started to divide world

First division in or from Europe

West Europe supports US

East Europe joins Soviet

Iron curtain divides East and West Europe

17th century: poles capture Kremlin

Next attack on Sweden

Germany invaded Soviet

Soviet troops by defending Nazis and Soviet West Regions are occupied

1945: US, Britain and SovietUnion met in Yalta, located along Black Sea coast of Crimean Peninsula

--Wanted to divide Germany

--Compensation of Germany for Soviet laws

--Stalin promised to hold elections in Eastern Europe

After war, Stalin ignored Yalta Agreement and established communist government

[Led to USSR dominance in Eastern Europe]

Communist government formed in Germany East and named as German Democratic Republic

US trie's to contain Soviets

1946- 47: President Truman planned a policy to contain Soviet [CONTAINMENT POLICY]

-To Stop Soviet influence

-To curb communism

Truman doctrine was first announced to help Turkey and Greece

To restrict Soviet influence

- **Soviet pressuring Turkey to allow Russian ships to freely flow from Turkish Straits-----(Join Black and Mediterranean sea)**
  - **Greece was with civil war (Greece government VS communist party.**
- **1946: Greece PM seeks help from US to resist communist power**
  - **Truman announced 400 million$ aid to Turkey and Greece.**
  - **Led to choas between US allies and USSR about Germany.**

Berlin Airlift

- **1948: France. Britain and US decided to withdraw their forces from Germany.**
  - **Based on Yalta agreement**
  - **Occupation zones are to form a nation.**
- **In response by Soviet, West Berlin made hostage.**
  - **It cut Berlin's highway, water and rail.**
  - **Allies will surrender west Berlin**
  - **Allies will leaves their idea to unify.**
  - **Allies will supply food and other needs to Berlin through air.**

May, 1949: Soviet surrender themselves.

- **This conflict led to cold war between US and Soviet union.**

Superpowers from Rival Alliances

1949: West European nations, Canada, US form military organization called NATO

1955: Warsaw Pact as a Soviet defense in Poland

Members of this pact are

East Germany

Czechoslovakia

Poland

Hungary

Romania

Bulgaria

Albanic

1961: Berlin Wall built and become as symbol of division between two rival camps

Threat of nuclear war

Soviet Union detonated its first atomic bomb on August 29th, 1949 at Semipalatinsk test site in Kazakhstan

1952: US testes its first hydrogen bomb

1953: Soviet Union also explodes it

Two countries invested more on nuclear weapons, which leads to arm's race

Cold war in skies

August, 1957: Sputnik [first unmanned satellite sent to space] with ICBM by Soviets

1958: US launches its first satellite

1960: US spy plane (U-2) was shot down by Soviets and captured its pilot which led to amid rise in cold war tensions

Conclusion

Coldwar was conflict between

communist state and democracy

Capitalism vs communalism

1991: Coldwar ended with disintegration of Soviet Union

Fall of USSR(1991)

- Introduction
- USSR born after October revolution
- 1922 : Formed by 4 Republics — Ukranian — Russian — Belarusian ,Trancaucasian

Internal weakness of USSR

- USSR was totalitarian states with one party system.
  - Only communist party
  - There was Russian dominance (term of language)
- Economy downfall
- Internal riots

External factors

- Due to USA propaganda, republics started coming out from USSR influence.

Events leading to Disintegration

- Dissolution starts when USSR last leader, gorbhachev come into power (1985)
    *Gorbhachev: Initiates policies for fast changes in Soviet.
    •Glasnost

-Political openess

- Eliminates Stalinist repression

- Other political parties allowed in election

And

- **Perestroika**
  - **Economic restructuring**
  - **Workers got better wages and conditions**
  - **Encourage foreign investment**
  - **Collapsed "Command economy" and fostered market economy.**
  - **Revolutions of 1989 and fall of Soviet union**
  - **Withdrawal of troops from Afghanistan.**
  - **Reduced Soviet military from Eastern Europe of Warsaw pact.**
  - **1989: 1st revolution in Poland by non- communist trade unions demanding free election.**
  - **Solidarity movement leaders got success.**
  - **1989, Nov 9: Communist and non communist Germany unification after fall of Berlin wall.**

    -"Velvet Revolution"—Overthrew communist government in Czechoslovakia.
  - **In Germany, Czech Poland, Hungary, Romania, Bulgaria led to downfall of communist government.**

Soviet Union Collapsed

- **By system Europe revolution and "Hand – off policy" of Gorbachev, independence movement started in Soviet republics.**

- **1990: Estonia**

  Lithuania} Baltic nations, declared independence

  Latvia

- **Gorbachev signed a treaty with republics**

- **To form decentralisated union giving greater autonomy to republic.**

- **Party members kept Gorbachev under house arrest and planned coup.**

Couple leaders declared state of emergency and military faced citizens to protect parliament

-- Coup was failed which was led by Boris Yelstin

--Gorbachev was freed

Gorbachev resigned from party general secretary, Realizing party can't be reformed

December 1st, 1991: Independence of Ukraine

USSR collapsed

December 8th, 1991: Yelstin with Belarus and Ukraine President signed a treaty to form union of republics, known as Commonwealth of Independent States

25th of December, 1991: Gorbachev resigned and USSR was formally dissolved and also believed that Cold War too ended

Non – Aligned Movement

History

- **1955: NAM origins in Bandung conference (Afro-Asian conference) in Indonesia.**

    - 23 Asian and 6 African countries participated.

    - 10 polices were declared to govern relations among countries (Bandung principles)

- 1961: NAM was 1st established in 1st Summit organised at Belgrade.

    - **Afganistan, Algeria, Yemen, Srilanka, Myanmar, cambdia, Congo, cuba, Cyprus, Egypt, Ethiopia, Gbano, Guninea, India, Indonesia, Iraq, Lebanan, Mali, Morocco, Nepal, Saudia Arabia, Somalia, Sudan, Syria, Yugoslavia participated.**

    Main role by Abdel Nassar, Kwamenkrumah, JLN, Ahmed, Sukarno, Josip Broz

    Founding fathers of NAM

Objective's of NAM

Self determination, national independence, states sovereignty, territorial integrity

Opposes----- Apartheid and imperialism

Keeping NAM countries far from super powers

Non interference in state affairs

Follow peaceful coexistence

Aim to make stronger United Nations

Democratization of international relations

Socioeconomic development

Equal footing

Political coordination

Principles

1st	·	Respect for human rights and principles of UN charter
2nd	·	Respecting every state's sovereignty, sovereign equality and territorial integrity
3rd	·	Recognition of equality among races religions, cultures and nations
4th	·	recognizing equality among dialouge promotion
5th	·	Promote and respect human rights, fundamental freedom
6th	·	Freely determine cultural, political, economic system without any intervention
7th	·	Reaffirm right to self determination
8th	·	Non-interference in states internal affairs
9th	·	Rejects government unconstitutional change
10th	·	rejects any attempt of regime change
11th	·	Condemned use of mercenaries in conflict situation

Role of NAM

- **Depicted great Solidarity**
- **Decolonization was also a pressure built by NAM**
- **NAM concerns on**
  - **1973: concept of "new international economics order" in Algiers conference.**
- **Promoted South- South and North- South cooperation**
- **Played a government role in maintaining the World peace and International security.**